Good Neighbours

Books by
Richard Gordon

Doctor in the House
Doctor at Sea
Doctor at Large
Doctor in Love
Doctor and Son
Doctor in Clover
Doctor on Toast
Doctor in the Swim
Doctor on the Boil
Doctor on the Brain
Doctor in the Nude
Doctor on the Job
The Captain's Table
Nuts in May
The Summer of Sir Lancelot
Love and Sir Lancelot
The Facemaker
Surgeon at Arms
The Facts of Life
The Medical Witness
The Sleep of Life
Good Neighbours

by

Mary and Richard Gordon

A Baby in the House

Good Neighbours

Suburbia Observed

Richard Gordon

HEINEMANN : LONDON

William Heinemann Ltd
15 Queen Street, Mayfair, London W1X 8BE
LONDON MELBOURNE TORONTO
JOHANNESBURG AUCKLAND

First published 1976
© Richard Gordon Ltd 1976

SBN 434 30243 0

Printed in Great Britain by
Cox & Wyman Ltd
London, Fakenham and Reading

To The Neighbours

Contents

1 *Coming of Age in Suburbia*

Twenty-one years ago I decided to follow the literary trend and emigrate to Jamaica. But we nested *en route* in north-west Kent for breeding, the facilities being foreseeably more reliable. We have moved once since – effortlessly, involuntarily and infuriatingly. The faceless bureaucrats of Bankside, unconfutably remote behind their stockade of floodlit columns at County Hall, whipped Kent from under my feet and made me live in BR1 2AX.

BR1 2AX! The words had the ring of the Gulag Archipelago. I had previously existed in Mr Jingle's heaven of apples, cherries, hops and women. Then it disappeared overnight, ten miles down the road to Hastings.

As a Kentish man, the source of my rate demands, driving licences and justice was Maidstone, a county town jostled by heavy-boughed orchards and fringed with hop-vines, right in the middle of the Garden of England. Its straggling High Street was full of pink-faced people with easygoing smiles, its shops seemed all grocers' and seedsmen's and chandlers', deliciously fragrant. Its summers were timed with a mellow, willow tick on one of the loveliest cricket grounds in the country. The Royal Navy guarded me at Chatham. The best oysters in the world bred

3

with unselfish vigour at Whitstable. And down the M2, Canterbury offered the most reliable spiritual inspiration.

Now my official orders, my demands for official cash, emanate from blind Furies in Greater London. As impersonally as the trains from its main line termini, which in their traditional drabness, dinginess, untidiness and overpriced begrudging facilities our whole capital is coming to resemble.

Had I defaulted on the rates in my pastoral days, I should have been locked in Maidstone's ragstone Georgian gaol, which still houses the better class of prisoner. Had I murdered my wife, I should have enjoyed the consolation of a fashionable trial in the Shire Hall, with a fanfare of trumpets and a nosegay for the judge, the mayor gold-chained in fur-edged scarlet and three-cornered hat, the sheriffs in knee-breeches, a massive mace and a turn-out of the Territorials. Now I should queue up with everyone else at the Old Bailey, where the clientele is manifestly growing more vulgarly sordid every session.

When Kent ebbed away as swiftly as a spring tide from the Goodwin Sands off the white cliffs of Dover, it exposed me to a cold and dampening awareness. I had been banished to live in the suburbs, for life.

A decade has passed. Now I love my suburb. As fondly as Gauguin loved Tahiti, Robert Louis Stevenson loved Samoa and Dr Schweitzer loved his leper colony in French Equatorial Africa.

'It is unnatural for an artist to live in a semi-detached villa and eat cottage pie cooked by a maid of all work,' wrote my fellow doctor W S Maugham from Cap Ferrat. But Maugham was a spark in the trailing clouds of Edwardian glory. When he made that remark in 1938, he was still forming beautiful crystals from the amorphous opinions of a society which knew its places, and kept them.

An artist with his heart set upon a semi-det today would be more likely to raise a laugh than a mortgage. Our maid of all work drives across three mornings a week in her Toyota, and we buy our cottage pie in convenience packs deep-frozen from Bejams. In the suburbs we are anyway inured to the sting of intellectual spit. It is impossible to find anything originally scathing or amusing to say about us, because it was all said before the 1930s finally exploded in everyone's faces.

*   *   *

Like the Australian nation, I have developed a touchingly blind pride in the outlandish place where I find myself living. BR1 2AX is my village. It stands on a gently rising, eastern-facing hillock and the upper levels of the property market. One of its bounds, to the east, is washed by the River Quaggy. This is one of London's lost rivers, like the Fleet, its banks long overgrown with a vegetation of bricks and mortar, gas-mains and railway lines. But it may still be glimpsed, tumbling between culverts as it runs like Alph through measureless caverns beneath Hither Green to a sunless sea at Deptford Creek.

To the south, we contemplate the fields of the most desperate and necessary victory in Britain's history, Biggin Hill. Just north, lies the famous spelaeological region of Chislehurst. On the West, the land rises to the telly mast atop Sydenham Hill, which every evening disseminates more entertainment than Shakespeare in his entire lifetime.

The architecture is unexpectedly international. Our houses would be at home in the poplar-spiked hills of Tuscany, the baked valleys of Andalucía or under the midnight suns of Lapland. Some of the split-levels would be familiar to cowboys sauntering bow-legged back to the ranch in the American West. Others are long and white with low-pitched roofs, delicately porched and porticoed, and might attract a knowing smile from any errant shade of an Old Southern gentleman. A few with azure tiles, ever-open green shutters and Snowcemmed exteriors, could have drawn a flutter of recognition from the world-weary lids of Somerset Maugham himself.

Anonymity is anathema in our roads. We would no more leave our house without a name than our dog. Many are a combination of the numeral and the arboreal – Two Elms, Three Oaks, Four Beeches. Or simply The Pines or The Firs, conifers enjoying eponymic popularity. Some gateposts express mysterious plurals, like Squirries, Twickets, Cratchetts. The only reason appears that the words would look even more stupid in the singular.

A substantial number of our homes are named after places at some considerable distance, Algarve, Strathspey, Lucerne, Lucknow, Windermere, Adelaide, São Paulo. This may represent enthusiasm for the cosy hypothesis, 'East West, Home's Best', or an economically strangled cry to return and live there instead of in BR1 2AX. Majorca is permissible among us, so is St. Helier, but not Balmoral. Chez Nous has never been observed in the area.

The streets are curved and well-treed, with many flowery culs-de-sac, the roadways liberally decorated with white paint, recalling the famous black-and-white mosaic pavement of Rossio Square in Lisbon. The grass of our village green survives, though badly nibbled by traffic. There are several pleasances and plunges, and numerous roadside gazebos furnished by London Transport. There are many inns.

We have an exuberantly self-confident Victorian church, flatteringly outsized to our needs, pale ochre, spired, clocked and clerestoreyed, robustly lightning-conductored, the churchyard prudently tarmacked for the worshippers' parking. It emits electronic peals on Sundays, and if you hold your funeral there the undertakers provide a special keener in a top hat to get you back into the main road traffic.

The water is pure, the air smokeless. I am content to report, as Gilbert White (1720–1793) of Selborne, 'The inhabitants enjoy a good share of health and longevity; and the parish swarms with children'.

* * *

The soil is gravel, and supports a variegated crop – pulses, radishes, tomatoes, rhubarb, marrows, spring onions. Since the winter of 1974, much grassland has been put under cultivation. The area is extensively wooded, with larch, laburnum, lilac, monkey-puzzles and yuccas.

Despite our elevation, and the soundly maintained

7

banks of the River Quaggy, there would appear danger of severe flooding. The apprehension of the inhabitants towards this disaster during the winter months is considerable, many of them preparing boats in their front gardens. Their concern is so lively, these craft are large enough to embark the whole family with ample stowage for their valuables, and need no more than the loosening of a tarpaulin for everybody to float away upon the rising waters and perpetuate life elsewhere, like the Ark.

We are rich in wildlife. Owls screech from the corpses of elms dead of the Dutch disease. Doves coo among the plastic ones on rooftops. The sparrow chirps cheerfully from the telly aerial, the gaily-waistcoated thrush grubs leatherjackets from the grass. The bright-eyed squirrel leaps from tree and drain-pipe everywhere, as mischievous and miraculously nimble as a hobgoblin. The hedgehog sleeps away his secret life, the mole makes mountainous hills on our lawn. The guinea-pig and gerbil are endogenous.

On a shining night in the season of the year, foxes slip from their earth on the Southern Region embankments. In the morning, the crisp, white, early lawn is printed with their spoor, and we shoot the backdoor bolts fearfully unless we hear the reassuring mewing of the cat.

There is sadly no hunting in the district. I must confess a sentimental, old-fashioned longing to witness a meet of The BR1 2AX in the car park of our local, top-hatted and pink-coated, mounted on the finest flesh of our extremely reasonably priced riding stables. Then to watch the hearty-greeting huntsmen toss down their stirrup cups of Babycham before clattering off with clamorous horn and exuberant shout, following a baying pack of rodent control officers along the departure platform and galloping up the main electrified line to Charing Cross.

I naturally respect the consciences of those who oppose foxhunting, as I respect the consciences of opponents to direct grant schools, private patients and Ascot week (generally the same people and for the same reason). As a traditionalist, I must demur that foxes are unpleasant and disruptive vermin. I hear every autumn bitter complaints from commuters, of foxes openly sneering at them from the frosty, golden open air, while they are jammed knee to knee in the morning trains to London.

The shooting is poor. The insect life is prolific, bees, midges, beetles, earwigs, greenfly. Of fish, the *Cyprinus auratus* is widely distributed. Our predominant fauna are cats and dogs. Allowing for wastage, a family will get through three or four of each in a suburban lifetime. Both species exist on a high-protein diet, but the dogs are fined ten pounds for performing naturally on the pavement. BR1 2AX is definitely not budgie country.

It is sad that we have no mute inglorious Hardy, no suburban Gilbert White, not even an indefatigably nosy Margaret Mead, to record our natural history. I have studied closely the people I went to live among. I have adopted their quaint customs, their distinctive modes of speech and dress, even their native food and drink. I have attempted to record

9

their daily movements, their household economy, their family structure. To classify their political system and their religious practices. To discover their feelings, their atavistic beliefs, their civilizing influences. This has not been easy among so shy and reticent a people, even for one now indistinguishable by the visitor from the natives.

I have approached my study of the country both anthropologically and biologically. But I aim no more than to present a simple story of suburban folk.

2 *A Year and a Day in the Suburbs*

Peregrine was my visitor from London. He is a smart fellow, with square glasses, a moustache wilting like a bar of chocolate in the sun, corduroy shoes and leather trousers, a pad in Chelsea and a job in public relations. He chaffed me on my possession of a watch and a calendar.

'Surely, me old darling,' Peregrine said, in that voice weary from continual subjection to the daily hectic whirl of the London Underground. 'You don't need such implements, not in *your* life. It makes not the slightest difference down here what hour or month it is. And it must be bleeding difficult to tell, anyway.'

I explained to my sharp urban friend, that was precisely why I required such *aides-memoire* to the passage of time. 'You city folk are obsessed with hours and minutes,' I chided him, kindly but assertively. 'Here in the suburbs, we can sit back on our patios and observe the sun's daily picket across the sky. And we appreciate each solar march from dawn to nightfall as part of his glorious, multi-hued procession from each year's frost-bitten, dusky start to its end under similar conditions.'

'Suppose the bleeding sun isn't shining, then?' he demanded, with that sourness which lies upon city dwellers like the mould on the overlooked Czecho-Slovakian gherkins.

'For the eye, and for the ear, of those among us who have sat at Mother Nature's dame school,' I reproved him gently, 'the season of the year and time of day is apparent from our immediate surroundings. Just as you sophisticated people discover them from the changing displays in Harrods windows or the Post Office speaking clock.'

I leant back in my gaily coloured deckchair, observing contentedly the sparrows disporting in the bird-bath against the lawn, under the well-creosoted trellis with the ramblers. Butch, our miniature poodle, lay newly clipped at my feet. Above my head spread the striped beach umbrella we had brought back from Fuengirola, stuck in its flowerpot of gravel. It was a glorious summer evening, the sun still high over the conical yew, the patio glowing in its nook beside the car port. We were sipping our gin-and-Slimlines, while the wife in the kitchen was preparing our dinner and listening to the Archers.

In a patient voice, I painted for Peregrine the subtle shading of the seasons in suburbia.

We know that spring has come, when the Atcos start chattering merrily to one another and the Tarpens screech happily in the hedgerows. The scritch-scritch of the hoe rises from the rose arbours, the milkman whistles as he clinks down his morning bottles, and we locate again the tennis markers on the lawn by jabbing all round with the hand-fork. The joyful vernal festival is upon us, of turning off the central heating and resetting the boiler time-switch for hot water only. In the lengthening evening sun, suburban men gossip over their fences, as for generation upon generation, about the impossibility of meeting the rate demands.

In summer, the tennis players perform their ritual dances, uttering their wild orgasmic cries. The dawn chorus of sparrows now rouses us, even before the lively hoots of the earliest electric train. From the sward comes the tangy fragrance of hormonal weed-killers, and in the evening the gentle rain droppeth from the Green Queen. When dusk begins to edge on midnight, the television screens shine with faint, bluish flicker to each other through the open picture windows, like mating glow-worms.

Come autumn, our village lies under a pall of smoke. How delightful are the passive pleasures of pyromania! We lean on our rubber rakes, in our wartime duffle coats, in our wellies patched by the children's puncture outfits, placidly watching the combustion of leaves ignited by yesterday's *Telegraph*. As we contemplate the billowy column, rising straight into the darkening teatime air like some released but benevolent genie, perhaps we give a thought to the ultimate incineration which awaits us all over at Beckenham Crematorium.

We squirt aerosols on the final marauding wasps, we gather in the plastic trug our last maggot-laden apples, we scrape a summer's cuttings from the Flymo and make chutney from the immutably green tomatoes. The early frosts rime the decorative iron-work and even glaze the bird-bath. They also sear enough vegetation to reveal the featherboarding which we meant to repair in the spring, and which still suggests a set of bad teeth.

Approaching winter chivvies the busy husband-man. Dahlias once blackened must be lifted, and laid carefully in Sainsbury's cardboard boxes next to the deep freeze in the garage. Beds must be re-planted with shrubs and roses from the garden centre. The tennis-netting is taken down, the car Bluecoled and garaged securely for the night.

When the cold frames have been finally frost-proofed, when the dog's tartan coat has been looked out from the loft and examined for moth-holes, when the electric blanket has been plugged-in with the Teasmade, and when the sodium lamps' amber gleam cheers the homecoming traveller through the chilly haze, then we can stretch our slippered toes towards the smokeless Gloco and relax in our cardi with our Cadbury's drinking chocolate over the winter schedules on the telly.

Soon we know that Christmas is coming, because of the drunks in the pubs.

*   *   *

As I finished my recital of the suburbanite's calendar, Peregrine took a drag at his fragrant Gauloise and tipped up his drained glass for the fourth occasion, in the hope of being offered another gin-and-Slimline.

For a moment he was silent. 'Man, you know how it all sounds? Like Hollywood in the 1920s,' he said, not entirely seriously. 'Or maybe the Roman Empire, just between the lovely decline and the fall.'

'Admittedly, the pastoral changes with our seasons may be simple,' I retaliated quite sharply from my deckchair. 'But they are only adjustments made to Nature, expressing an ecology which is infinitely complex.'

'You're joking?'

'Let me describe to you a typical day in Suburbia.'

He made no reply, just crushed out his Gauloise in the souvenir ashtray from Rimini and tipped his empty glass rapidly twice. I proceeded.

I depicted each village morning, beginning with a reveille of burglar alarms, sleepily triggered by inhabitants blearily groping for the newspapers on the mat. At seven, the Post Office sends a man round to rev up a pop-popping two-stroke under the bedroom windows, to wake up the remaining sluggards. The first hour of the day tightly compresses the most violent activity. Dogs and cats are let out and in. The bathroom is occupied and reoccupied with the split-second timing of a Feydeau farce. Traffic bulletins must be absorbed from the transistor while the attention is simultaneously engaged in eating or shaving or reading the newspaper or shouting at the children, on some mornings all four together. The whole house is vibrant with the flush of toilets.

The hour ends in a sudden and amazing climax. All the males hurriedly flee. They leave the women with Tony Blackburn and utterly unprotected. This regular daily abandonment finds no parallel in any anthropological study known to the world. The males' only safeguard is a makeshift chastity belt of prying, under-school-age children.

Predators move in swiftly. Milkmen, delivery-men, dustmen to redistribute the household rubbish along the front path. Repairmen, whose numbers equal the square of the number of labour-saving gadgets inside (*The Law of Dynamic Obsolescence*). Men with tatty vans, selling eggs and manure guaranteed fresh from the farm. Men with a load of tar left over from the last job, eager to tarmac the drive cheap. Pollsters and Jehovah's Witnesses. Men giving good prices for old silver. And window cleaners, all with the blood of George Formby flowing in their veins.

Among these predators appears from time to time the local medicine man. He enjoys a different and enviable status.

The medicine man's holy aura, his fearsome power, his essentiality in ill-health, his necessity in even the simplest activities and plans of suburban life, afford him the unquestioning reverence and even abasement of his flock. The medicine man can enter any house he wishes, without even setting a definite time in advance. The woman can be entirely alone, in bed, stark naked. The medicine man simply rings the doorbell and goes upstairs to the bedroom.

Such is the awesomeness of the medicine man that the husband readily accepts this conduct. He may even suggest it. He would not generally do the same with, for instance, an insurance broker who was a fellow-member of the golf club.

The medicine man carries his bag of charms, strange and frightening designs in metal, glass and plastic. He will display some of his charms in the

18

bedroom, but never all of them at once. The case contains also his *ju-ju*, which he always uses while weaving his spells.

The ju-ju closely resembles a water-diviner's cleft stick, and is employed for the same purpose. The medicine man wears it round his neck. Though the ju-ju is primarily to detect the evil in his suppliants, the medicine man affords it a secondary role in the performance of ritualistic, and sometimes threatening, gestures towards them.

His mystique and frightening potency are enough in themselves to reduce his votaries to dumb intimidation or terror. He has no necessity to perform ritual dances or intone chants in the course of his duties. But his magic spells are pronounced in tones of considerable and sometimes crushing solemnity.

The indispensable item of the medicine man's equipment is his mask. It carries an expression of amiable, bland impassiveness, resembling the smiling Buddhas of the Ming period during the sixteenth century. The mask is to shield his inner feelings. They can only be speculated upon by the women when the medicine man lays hands – without encouragement, or even much invitation – upon the most intimate portions of their bodies. The husband does not object to this, and it is thought that the woman does not, either.

Still wearing his mask, playing with his ju-ju, the medicine man hears all the deepest, and often the otherwise unuttered, confidences of the village. He is the only suburban man, apart from her husband, with whom a suburban woman can freely, unguiltily and conveniently share her innermost secrets. And often the husband does not get to know the half of it.

The medicine man is careful never to form an attachment to any particular woman in the village. Nor does he give her the remotest impression that such would be possible. 'Dodge the grab when they try to hold your hand,' a seasoned medicine man of the suburbs told me. 'I advise them all to join the Weight Watchers. It seems to turn them off.'

Persistence with this cautiously distant, but doubtless infuriating, attitude allows the medicine man to enjoy the intimacy of all the available women in the village.

*   *   *

I had reached no further with this account of a single, and to myself fascinating, day in the life of our village, when my lady wife appeared smiling on the patio for her customary Campari, announcing that dinner was shortly to be served. We had sacrificed a chicken to the stranger, in the way of the simple natives in Dahomey (Geoffrey Gorer, *Africa Dances*). As we entered our dining-room with the green flock wallpaper and bracket lights, I was pleased to notice that the wife had served with it, in deference to Peregrine's sophistication, frozen runner beans instead of her usual peas. The repast opened with freshly thawed prawns in Heinz salad cream and afters was ices.

My house is among the oldest in BR1 2AX. It is of russet Edwardian brick, tile-hung and shingle-roofed, its chimneys as graceful as a pianist's fingers pointing smokeless to the sky, built amid a nest of scaffold-poles in sand-tubs by ragged trousered philanthropists. The dormer window of my attic workroom views like a watchtower the gardens and glades, the shrubberies and copses (subject to tree-preservation orders), the rooftops and greenhouses, the barbecues and climbing-frames, the eternal, measured flashing of the traffic lights and the twinkling direction-indicators which comprise our busy village. Its sounds have grown as familiar to me as the beat of the sea to a fisherman. Even with the windows firmly shut, I hear the rattle of the electric trains like hastening steel skeletons, the strident wail of police-car and fire-engine, the summer transistor warbling its tuneless note, the competitive snarl of young men's motor-bikes, and the lively chatter of schoolchildren, playing their boisterous little sexy games and lighting their fags once out of school.

I have seen twenty-one years of our country's history reflected in the usually expressionless face of BR1 2AX. After the servants had departed, and before the electronically programmed wash had arrived, houses living in companionship to mine honeycombed themselves into awkward little flats. In the property boom of the 1960s, much Edwardian brickwork was demolished, house and garden was replaced with a new town of Chartreuse-coloured roofs and white plastic clapboard.

The fences were down, front lawn was confulent with front lawn. The abodes stood as close as volumes on a shelf, conversation in any lounge becoming confusingly mingled with that in the next (*The*

Ayckbourn Effect). Neighbourliness was brought to the village at last, by the property developers. But your true-bred suburban man is a Conservative fellow, suspicious of new-fangled inventions, and the neighbourliness has been used as little as the pre-installed bathroom ultraviolet sun lamp or the heatless imitation coal fire.

Now there is a property slump again. Times resemble that winter when I first viewed the residence, tramping up a frosted drive to discover a tangled garden and that someone had pinched the lead from the roof. Estate agents' boards once more droop and rot over the fences, as forlorn as ensigns from the taffrails of laid-up ships. BR1 2AX may be on its way to a ghost village, dilapidated and unmown, populated by a few hammered stockbrokers, bankrupt company directors and underwriters for whom the Lutine Bell has tolled.

So bleak an end recently decided us to move. I wrote for particulars of houses in the near-by villages of TN 9 and TN 13, even as far afield as RU 8. Only one residence appealed to me. Its attractive features included charming L-shaped oak-panelled hall, sun-trap patio, double garaging, mature garden, sep. W C and spacious receps. The price was exactly what we could afford. I discovered that I had picked up the estate agent's description of my own house. We bought it.

We shall never get to Montego Bay. I can make myself as happy in suburbia as Robinson Crusoe on his desert island, because I have a suburban mind. This is cause for neither shame nor denial. The commuter-computed suburbs of London run from Broadstairs to Bath, which is convenient for Bristol, and from Worthing to Leamington Spa on the edge of Birmingham. The residents of both Philadelphia and Baltimore live in the suburbs of both New York and Washington. Legislators commute as easily from Canberra to Sydney as from Ottawa to Montreal. The European Economic Community had to be formed because Brussels lies in the suburbs of all the principal towns of North Europe.

Millions of Americans have been uprooted from their homes to live in Zip Code, a place akin to Dodge City. French peasants have been forced into *Boîtes*, which are nightclubs. Rugged Australians from the outback are penned like their own sheep into Boxes, and South Africans scattered across the veldt even done up into numbered Bags.

The world's suburbs extend unbroken from Funabashi north of Tokyo to Sea Point near Cape Town, from St Kilda south of Melbourne to Whytecliff outside Vancouver, via Bogorodskoye on the outskirts of Moscow. We are all suburbanites now. Even from Cap Ferrat, you can get a bus equally easily to Nice or Monte Carlo.

3 *The Life Cycle of the Suburbanite*

The life cycle of the suburbanite is best understood from the biological rather than the anthropological standpoint. It has two distinct forms, resembling the mosquito-borne *plasmodium* parasite causing malaria·

Sir Ronald Ross (1857–1932) demonstrated at his laboratory in Calcutta how the microscopic *plasmodium* exists in the blood of infected man and in the stomach of the spotted-winged *Anopheles* mosquito, in an *asexual* and *sexual* form.

In the suburbanite, the *asexual* cycle occurs from Monday to Friday. The *sexual* cycle is from Friday night to Monday morning.

During his asexual phase, the male suburbanite is difficult to observe. He wakes, and feeds briefly from coloured packets set overnight among the Denby ware. Male, female and young seem at this time largely indifferent to one another, though there may be bursts of threatening behaviour, interspersed with pecking at the cereal food. The eating would seem only a *displacement activity*, like the bouts of feeding which intersperse the fighting of cockerels and other aggressive animals.

The male then abruptly abandons his territory. He is often absent until the approach of darkness. The female does not normally stray far from the abode. From Monday to Friday she does not set out to attract other males.

The feeding of the female is interesting during the asexual phase. In the middle of the day she prepares herself a small meal of lettuce-leaf, starched-reduced crispbread, fat-free yoghurt and a cup of black coffee. She eats this alone, at the formica-topped table in the kitchen. This does not take her long, and afterwards all is washed up and tidied away diligently.

About twenty minutes later, she opens the fridge door and extracts a large hunk of Irish Cheddar, which she eats rapidly, standing up. A further ten minutes elapse, and she removes the lid from a circular tin to cut herself a substantial slice of dairy cream sponge sandwich. Five minutes later, she un- wraps a bar of Cadbury's fruit and nut from its silver paper. The crumbs of this supplementary nutriment are always gathered carefully and sprinkled down the Wastemaster. She may end the meal by opening the cupboard in the lounge and pouring herself a slug of vodka. This is invariably followed by a mouthwash and gargle in the bathroom upstairs.

The female forages during the asexual phase, generally in the earlier part of the day. Intensive preening occurs before she leaves the abode. This behaviour is unvariable, even though she is going only a hundred yards to order some item like a load of smokeless coke.

As there are no longer males of her species re- maining in the territory, this preening, too, may be a displacement activity. But it may be important for her to present a good appearance before other females, who during the sexual phase are possibly competing for the available males.

Foraging follows an elaborate pattern. She collects small amounts from various places, to any of which she may return on two or more occasions during the day. Though she regards this as a tiresome and even exhausting performance, it may be simply a time-occupying one, or a means of avoiding less agreeable activities, like ironing the sheets or Harpic-ing the loo.

Once a week she forages farther afield and returns with a variety of foodstuffs and materials for building the abode. She obtains also a talisman, a strip of white paper some two inches wide which may be over a foot long, inscribed with figures. This must never be shown to the male.

No foraging is ever done on foot, even for such unburdensome items as sewing-needles or postage stamps.

* * *

The female also leaves the abode for maintenance activities, taking the animals to the vet, the heat-retaining rollers to the electrician's or the children to the medicine man. Her only other foray is to a *coffee morning*.

These are of two types, (1) the purposeful and (2) the purposeless.

(1) *Purposeful* coffee mornings are a gathering of thirty to fifty females to raise money for people with schizophrenia, heart disease, cystic fibrosis, leprosy and other specific afflictions. Or they may be held

for the accumulation of discarded clothes and simple household implements for dispatch overseas to Oxfam.

Oxfam is one of the eternally emergent and unescapably under-privileged nations on the African continent. Though the temperature there is always high, and rain falls almost continually, the soil is so poor that nothing will grow. The inhabitants are therefore forced to depend for food and clothing, and for their meanest luxuries, on what may be spared from even so impoverished a country as Britain. These inhabitants would appear from their photographs in the newspapers to pass their lives in unsmiling melancholy, which they attempt to relieve by continually breeding children.

The suburban female applies to her gesture towards Oxfam considerable thought. She must not risk the suspicion of meanness. Nor of impecuniosity, a much worse proclivity in the eyes of the community. Her mind becomes a simultaneous equation. She balances a generous offering against the anger of the male when he discovers it (which may be a considerable time later). And an offering of less value against the calculations of the other females, who are able instantly to price any article down to the nearest 1p.

No direct accusation of either parsimony or poverty is made during a coffee morning to the female herself. On the contrary, any gift whatever, even a frayed Old Alleynian tie, a worn-through pair of sneakers or a friable Spanish straw hat are received with warm expressions of gratitude and appreciation.

The ritual is for each donation to be assessed later by the other females among themselves, and their remarks relayed *in toto* by one of their number over the telephone almost instantly.

The female faces the further complication that her offering, though patently of good value and in sound repair, might indicate some lapse or even vulgarity in taste, which is best kept concealed inside the family. She would prefer to stay all morning isolated in her abode than display before her peer-group a see-through black nylon nightie with delicate lace at the bust, seductive perforated bra, French tights with open crutch or Swedish ones with no bottom, or even waterproof garments for adults, as advertised in the national Press.

Such strong psychological and economic pressures may force the female to give away cheerfully some almost new and cherished garment of her own. But she exercises much ingenuity to avoid censure from both her fellow females and her own male. Clothes no longer of use to her husband, through changing social conventions or obesity, may be sacrificed at a coffee morning with impunity. The inhabitants of Oxfam may be readily recognized by any traveller to their steamy and barren land by many being attired in tight-fitting dinner-jackets, or tail suits and stiff-fronted shirts, with grey top hats or the peaked caps of various cricket clubs. The women of Oxfam today wear miniskirts, hot pants, suspender-belts and anything from Biba's.

Our females enjoy one indulgence during the ordeal of a coffee morning. Any article of clothing, in any state of repair, is acceptable without demur if it originates from *M & S*.

This is a sales organization founded by Karl Marx (1818–1883), the German father of International Socialism, and Herbert Spencer (1820–1903), the English philosopher, anthropologist and economist. The genius of these two men evolved an emporium where quality was combined with equality, at most reasonable prices, which so appealed to the fundamental spirit of British liberalism that it is today enthusiastically patronized without shame by members of all classes. It is appropriate that these two powerful influences on our country's life, whose names are inevitably spoken as one, should be buried on the east side of Highgate New Cemetery opposite one another (C Bailey, *Famous London Graves*).

The donation of household appliances is less trying to the female's intellect. She often accumulates a store of them in the loft of the abode, awaiting forthcoming coffee mornings. The inhabitants of sodden and starving Oxfam, in their evening dress, can at least enjoy playing with their unfunctioning transistor radios, or their packs of cards and jigsaw puzzles slightly incomplete, or reading their sets of Thackeray and Thomas Carlyle, before mounting their kiddie-karts to call on their neighbours and watch 9-inch TV while listening to the 78 record-player.

The business of a coffee morning, like the coffee, is finished well before the morning itself. The rest of the time is filled with animated conversation. By convention, it is strictly limited to the three topics which all the women present have in common. This is a civilized concept, that none may feel at a loss for words.

The three subjects are—

(1) *The Washing Machine*.

Talk is generally further restricted to its numerous breakdowns, which are recounted in a humorous manner, the speaker being assured of sympathetic laughter from her audience.

(2) *Education of the Young*.

This subject is never treated humorously. Indeed, any statement is received with expressions of gloom and despair. It is a topic concentrating family economics and social status as intensely as the garments produced for sale. The difference lies in a permissiveness for all the females to admit openly the impossibility of affording private education for their young beyond the end of the current academic term.

All declare freely – their countenances assuming a look of abject horror – that offspring deprived of a normal education will stray into a *stateschool*. These are institutions preying on the young, for their forced instruction in crime, violence, and rebellion. They were first described by Dickens (1812–1870) in *Oliver Twist*.

No obliquy attaches to such a tragic prognostication by any female, the stateschool being recognized as an enemy installation against which the entire tribe can combine (cf Inland Revenue, Trade Unions, Socialism, Oil Sheikhs, Traffic

Wardens, Spanish Hoteliers, Pop Concerts, British Rail and Eddie Waring).

(3) *Gynaecology.*

There is no restriction on the anatomy or pathology discussed. All women in suburbia acquire a sound knowledge of this interesting medical subject from puberty onwards. The talk is well-informed, and conducted in clinical detail which would pass at meetings of the Royal College of Obstetricians and Gynaecologists in Regent's Park.

Each female is required, shortly after joining her peer group, to reveal at a coffee morning her complete and detailed gynaecological history. One of the longer established members of the group, who may be older, is obliged to notice any points of similarity with her own gynaecological experiences, and thereupon retell them to the others. In this way, all the females' gynaecology gets a regular airing.

Difficulties may arise when gynaecological reminiscences slide into sexual ones, clearly a simple transition. The change of subject is welcomed by the group, but the woman will generally end her story abruptly if tantalizingly. Such restraint is always accepted uncomplainingly by the remainder, who can never be too sure if it was their own husband involved.

(2) *Purposeless* coffee mornings are almost indistinguishable from the purposeful ones.

*   *   *

The free bandying about of the females' gynaecology only emphasizes that coffee mornings are an

34

entirely asexual activity. They may be seen in two variants—

(1) *The Sherry Morning*.

Sherry is served in place of coffee, because more money is required to be raised. The sherry is always dispensed in small amounts, and generally Cyprus.

(2) *The Tennis Morning*.

Summers only. Four or more females gather to play tennis, and though they may appear in short pleated skirts, white openwork tops, frilly knickers and centre court hair-dos, the occasion is somewhat sad, because there can be no males present.

A slightly different variation is the *Tribeswomen's Guild*, an association of women to eat an asexual lunch (chicken with salad in summer, with rice in winter). They are addressed by persons of importance, and afterwards ask intelligent questions. Outings are arranged to amateur theatricals, or to the afternoon performances of repertory players. Though a woman's more reliable, if unpublicized, source of local theatre tickets is the newsagent, who gets them every week for putting the showcard in his window.

Women's Lib is not a problem in suburbia.

Communication with others occurs only during the woman's asexual phase, towards the middle of the afternoon.

The traditional means for neighbours to exchange views on topics of mutual interest, or on the world in general, is across the back fence. In suburbia, this is sometimes possible for the male, but never for the female. She will speak to her female neighbour only by telephone, even if their houses are so closely adjacent that remarks enunciated clearly in the lounge with the window open can be heard distinctly in the lounge next door (see *Ayckbourn Effect*).

The female does not telephone the neighbouring female on any specific subject. Or rather, she picks some specific subject – the cat's ailments, difficulties with the young, vagaries of the front-opening automatic – to start a conversation with an invitation of advice, which both parties know she would have no intention whatever of following.

The discussion shortly becomes free-ranging, covering the habits of the male, all the other tribes-women and of course gynaecology. The talk may continue for an hour or more, for which contingency the female equips herself before sitting down at the instrument with a cup of tea and a tin of sweet biscuits.

The asexual phase is not a healthy one for the suburban female, when she is subject to headaches, feelings of afternoon prostration, discontent, self-torment, boredom, frustration and fantasies about Rex Harrison (b 1908).

4 Tribal Rites and Customs

Reproduction in the suburbs occurs at week-ends. As with all species of the animal kingdom, it produces marked and even violent changes in behaviour and appearance.

With the onset of the *sexual* phase, the male and female dress more luridly and loosely. The male during his asexual phase wears garments of priest-like severity. But on Saturday morning he decks himself in a canary-yellow crew-neck sweater, brown suède jacket, jeans, dark glasses and crêpe soles. This indicates that he is ready to reproduce.

The observer obtains from both male and female during the onset of the sexual phase an impression of light-hearted luxuriation in their habitat. This is at variance with exchanges conducted at night, or particularly at early morning, during the asexual phase. At such times, violent curses may be called by the male upon the abode, the village, the tribe, and even upon his own female, or at least her relatives. Now the male seems to express with his every action a Panglossian contentment with his lot. The abrupt change of habit pattern occurring on Friday nights – the withdrawal of male exertion and female secretiveness – seems to induce a state of euphoria.

This contentment with the environment is

particularly marked by the refurbishing activities of the male upon the abode itself. All the males of our village, whatever their occupations during the asexual phase – cost accountants, marketing managers, tax consultants, conveyancing solicitors and suchlike – in their sexual phase show a fierce pride, a pugnacity, over their powers as home-builders. Suburban man having risen above simple tools like the hammer and chisel, which have barely changed since the Iron Age, they accumulate a battery of Black and Deckers with which to rip the plaster off the walls. This activity is probably a vestige of man's sexually attractive prowess on the field of hunt or battle.

On the Saturday morning, there is often some reversal of roles between the male and female. The male will go shopping, with a basket on a stick with little wheels (though this may be only a device for meeting other females). He afterwards invariably goes to drink.

Early in the sexual phase the female paradoxically busies herself with the housework. This is comparable to the behaviour of the female dove, in whom the sight of the sexually aroused male causes hormonal changes making her ready for nest-building (Aubrey Manning, *An Introduction to Animal Behaviour*).

Housework is an activity normally performed irregularly during the week, always in solitude, wearing an old dress with bedroom slippers and smoking a cigarette. It consists in pulling up the bed, running the bath-taps, Hoovering the wall-to-wall carpeting downstairs, and stuffing anything which has been hanging about dirty more than three days into the front-loading automatic. It takes on each performance eight minutes.

The male attends the garden, mowing, cutting and clipping vigorously, then spraying everything with powerful chemicals.

The behaviour patterns of both male and female fit into the grand design of the suburb's sexual phase, being preparatory to accepting outsiders into the abode. This is itself a *display activity*. The social gradient of suburbanites is determined by the *Coefficient of Material Expansion*, which equals the sum of the cubic capacities at the abode plus that of all labour-saving gadgets therein and of the cars (RAC rating), multiplied by the square of the screen of the colour television set.

*   *   *

As with other creatures, the sexual activity of suburbanites is closely associated with feeding habits.

It is interesting that the *dinner party* has become vestigial, the cost of luxury food having grown beyond the suburbanite's grasp, as bananas beyond the short-necked giraffe which is now extinct and found in fossils. It can be traced as the *wine and cheese party*, but this too has degenerated from Camembert and Chianti to Double Gloucester and Double Diamond. *Sunday drinks* survives, to fill the focal period of the sexual cycle, between finishing the colour supplements and sitting down to the overdone roast.

Drinks at noon on Sundays is the pacemaker from

which the heartbeat of our village's social life originates. It occurs in the lounge in winter, on the patio in summer. A different couple open their homes each week, for exactly the same among us to gather together in the sight of St Augustine Barnett, saviour of the middle classes.

A changing venue is useful, in giving the illusion that we have found something new to talk about. Village conversation is necessarily limited. The elements of our world are always the same, only slightly rearranged from week to week, a kaleidoscope with dull-coloured glass. We discuss our young and our gardens, fondly but never sentimentally. We lament that everything is much worse than it was – gas from the North Sea, the beer, English cricket, the FT Index. But we are not parochial. We find ourselves soon discussing the burning social question of our times, why the bloody workers should always get it their own way.

In BR1 2AX we are politically highly sensitive. The great statesmen of the age have passed among us. Ted Heath stands near-by, and has edged even nearer since Bexley turned a paler shade of blue. Margaret Thatcher once slept down the road. Each General Election in the Super years brought Mr Harold Macmillan to our Town Hall, to oversee the assessment of his huge majority with the assistance of his fellow-candidates – including poor Mr Gerald Kaufman, later consoled as Mr Wilson's *éminence rouge* – some of whom even presumed to speak to him.

Our favourite politician is Winston Churchill, to whom death was but a trifling setback. We still sniff the whiff of his cigar smoke, we straighten our arthritic spines at his phrases. We see the world still through the eyes of war. Our country is under Socialist occupation, the British Government of 1976 is to us the French Government of mid-1940, created only for a surrender to our enemies which was swift, efficient and abject. Mr Wilson was our Pétain, Mr Foot our Laval. Our finest hour goes on for ever. Unfortunately, there does not seem much chance of D-Day.

We are a tight-knit group on Sunday mornings, but not a monolithic one. Most of us are breasting the currents – which may be icy or pleasantly warm – at various depths in the increasing fathoms of middle age. Quite a number of us still gambol on its nearer shore. To some of us, our wives turning us on at night has come to refer to the electric blanket. A few have become Senior Citizens, but like Mr Wedgwood Benn they have renounced the title.

We are snobbish. But so is everybody, socially above or below us. The aristocrat feels silently superior to the businessman. The businessman to the worker. The worker to the immigrant. Snobbery is the cement of society. Everyone indulges in it, except the one at the bottom who gets squashed by the weight.

*   *   *

As the effect of the gin wears on and that of the deodorant wears off, our Sunday parties become decorously drunken and subduedly sexy. Our males are of reasonable physique, clean and whiskered.

43

Our women possess a sound standard of beauty, with slim or sturdy figures and excellent teeth. At the acme of their sexual phase on Sunday mornings they can exert a powerful attraction for the male. During particularly high suburban festivals – for example, those held on Sundays towards the winter solstice – I am even reminded of those parties described by Paul Gauguin (1848–1903) at Tahiti in his *Noa Noa*, published in 1901. 'The men sing, while the women with rhythmical movements of their arms and legs imitate the love game to which they are inciting the men, and which will begin as soon as it is night'.

I must emphazise that these activities in suburbia are but faint tracings of those performed in Polynesia (to give one distinction, our women's breasts are never completely bared). But with experience, the observer can detect the subdued voluptuousness in the females' movements. The men sing only seldom, and then quietly in a melancholy and sentimental fashion, usually sitting down.

The tribal gathering, the sexual phase itself, reaches its climax with all the males performing displays of tenderness towards all the women. This is achieved with a highly ritualized embrace. A kiss is offered upon the cheek or the nose. It may *sometimes* be upon the mouth. It is accompanied by a simple hug, without high-pressure body-contact. It lasts three seconds.

To exceed these conventions may excite displeasure from the mates of both embracers, and certainly amused comment from the group. Though tribal etiquette is outrun, often excessively so, if the mates are elsewhere in the host's abode, and possibly up to exactly the same thing.

Immediately after the kissing ceremony, the party disperses. All that has occurred during the whole Sunday ritual is a complicated striking of attitudes in which no contact is established, perhaps best compared with the courtship dance of the wandering albatross (*Diomeda exulans*) in South Georgia.

There is little organized wife-swapping in suburbia. Certainly less than reported in such American suburbs as Peyton Place. It is unnecessary, the females all being so similar in appearance, outlook, speech and inhibitions.

The remainder of the sexual phase is dormant. Male and female sleep during the afternoon in their own abode, not together on the marriage-bed, but separately on a couch or chair wherever they happen to drop. They wake generally before nightfall, when other characteristics of the asexual cycle already begin to appear. They show less arousal towards one another, and seem already influenced by the instincts which keep them separated for almost half of each coming twenty-four hours. The precision with which exactly the same behaviour is reproduced each succeeding Monday morning is remarkable.

The number of offspring produced by the suburbanite is disappointingly small. They would seem infertile creatures, and there is a good cause for their preservation by law.

5 Totems and Taboos

Totem worship is practised universally in suburbia.

A totem may be defined as *Some animal or object containing the spirit of the tribal god, worshipped with conventional religious rites and symbolic of the group itself.*

Freud (1856–1939) goes further, believing the totem to represent the father, slain to obtain possession of his women by the sons, who are afterwards overcome with guilt. The totem is thus a father figure, and helps to keep down incest.

All these functions of the totem are exercised in my own suburban village.

As Sir James Frazer (1854–1941) indicated in his *Totemism* of 1887, tribal totems are of two sorts, *clan* totems and *sex* totems. Frazer's observation is amply confirmed by my own research. The natives of our village worship both totems, the clan totem during their asexual phase from Monday to Friday, the other in their sexual phase from Friday night to Monday morning.

The clan totem may be found in all abodes, without exception. It occupies the best room, and the best position in the room. It is kept clean and carefully polished by the female, and protected from all possible damage. The totem takes precedence over all other objects and beings in the room, and subjugates both the conversation and the attention of anyone entering it. Totemism occurs in the evening, about six o'clock, and is linked with the feeding habits.

Evening feeding itself provides an interesting study in the complex behaviour-patterns of the suburbanite. Each family implies to all others in the tribe that the male feeds in the later evening, consuming an elaborate meal of which the preparation has occupied the female during the entire latter half of the day. They suggest that it is offered and partaken with some ceremony, and accompanied by the sacrament from St Augustine Barnett. It is invariably referred to as 'dinner'.

This is a *pretence-display* activity. The meal is in reality chops shifted from the deep-freeze in the garage to the eye-level grill as the male is entering the abode, served with reconstituted mash and a bottled sauce, accompanied by Mackeson's stout and called 'supper' within the family. Kippers, a packet of Wall's sausages or baked beans on toast may be substituted. The Good Shepherd makes a frequent appearance. But tea is never drunk. The meal would then become 'high tea', which if known to the neighbours would excite contempt of a viciousness demanding instant emigration to another district.

Totemism often begins while the meal is still in progress. The family continue to eat automatically and unseeingly, as they enter the trancelike state of devotion.

The clan totem is analagous to the *sarn prapoom*,

the dovecote-like 'spirit house' which is found outside all buildings in Thailand. Its function is to conjure up a series of images, some of real persons, others of persons representing non-existent persons. Both these visions – whether the genuine beings or the imitators – may be of persons living or dead. Reverence of the totem would seem to be a form of ancestor worship, some of the persons appearing, particularly on Sunday afternoons and very late at night, having been dead some considerable time.

The whole family form a semi-circle, sitting in silence devoutly facing the totem for the entire evening. The rite is regularly interrupted by small, inconsequential episodes akin to the mediaeval miracle plays. They depict fantastic situations and achievements, and last two or three minutes. This is so hot refreshment may be sought or physical needs eased without missing any of the liturgy. It is known as the *T P Interval*.

Worship continues until the family feel an over-whelming desire to sleep. Sometimes, they wake to find the spirits have departed.

*　　　*　　　*

The simple people of my village believe all these ghosts to be real, even those which are clearly presented by the totem as non-existent. Much of their daily conversation is occupied with talk of the ghosts, of their doings and feelings. The folk often apply to the ghosts their own earthy predicaments and problems, speculating how these shadowy figures might solve them. The more familiar ghosts become well-established members of the family circle. This is how they are always spoken of, and sometimes to.

The more important spirits conjured by the totem are afforded great reverence. Though the worshippers may turn against them suddenly and savagely, as men against any god who fails to deliver the expected goods. These powerful spirits are sometimes observed walking the earth, when they are subjected to the profoundest abasement and wonder. The ghost world is more real to our natives than the concrete one they inhabit. This may be an unhealthy form of necromancy, or simply because the real world is so insufferably boring.

The tribal totem has a double function as an oracle, which is believed unquestioningly. Its prophets make announcements regularly during the evening service. The more pious worshippers believe that these prophets in some way control the events of which they speak.

About once a year, the totem presents a person of the real world, with some message of grave import from the beyond. But these are confused by the worshippers with the numerous non-existent spirits, and paid little regard, as they are neither colourful nor interesting to watch.

The size and type of the totem is of great importance to the status of the family. There are two sorts, plain and coloured. In a comparatively prosperous village like BR1 2AX, the display of a coloured totem is essential to enjoy social tolerance, much less esteem.

The Government conducts an annual offertory for

the spirits. Some worshippers avoid making their donation, but if discovered are exposed to tribal ridicule. The totem itself is acquired through a complicated system of regular offerings, which the family will face starvation to pay. The totem's removal through default is a social disaster as consequential as indulging in high tea.

Ours is a deeply religious community, worshipping regularly every night during the asexual phase, and often into the sexual phase as well. Sometimes the totem becomes unwell, causing anguish in the family greater than the affliction of its own members, and their summoning its acolyte for ministration more urgently than ever the medicine man.

*　　*　　*

Because of the biological changes induced by the altering life-cycle on Friday nights, the other totem is worshipped only by the man.

On Sunday morning, the males may be seen religiously cleaning their sexual totems. The more devoted males abase themselves to the totem, lying prone on the ground beneath it. Some even thrust their heads into its gaping jaws. They propitiate the totem with gifts – small square cushions, sheepskin rugs, pendulous ornaments of all sorts, doggies with electric eyes. They decorate it richly with holy medallions, or magic letters like *G B* or *G T*. They often attach to it a text, as once the custom to the statues of saints. These generally say, *No to Nationalization*, *Pick an English Cox* or *Don't Blame Me I Voted Conservative*. A new sex totem is proclaimed by the rubric *Running In. Sealink* is acceptable, but not *We Saw the Lions of Longleat.*

Each sexual totem is authenticated by an official code number, only the final letter of which is regarded as significant. A man is judged much from the size and splendour of his sex totem by his peers, and by the tribal women too.

As further observed by Sir James Frazer, 'The sex totem seems to be still more sacred than the clan totem; for men ... will fiercely defend their sex totem against any attempt of the opposite sex to injure it.'

Such pugnacity extends in suburbia to any attack – or apparent attack – by anyone whatever.

The sex totem can communicate only by uttering a single raucous note or by repeatedly flashing its eyes, both of which the affronted male will evoke readily. Should the attack be pressed home, the male will verbally berate the owner of the other totem, or even offer physical violence. As the other owner invariably retaliates, fierce passions swiftly become aroused, with a great deal of shouting. But as neither party can accept blame for the attack without humiliating loss of honour, such totem assaults, though commonplace, end only in widespread confusion.

The female too may possess a sex totem. Hers is much smaller than the male's, unfurbished and in poor repair, not regaled by offerings. It is never worshipped, even by the females themselves. The male deliberately keeps his female's sexual totem in such poor state, that his own may appear to shine the brighter. The female enjoys use of the male sex totem at the male's condescension. The female may *never* take charge of his sex totem while the male is present, even if he is too drunk to see the kerbstones. A female who damages her male's sexual totem may face banishment.

*　　　*　　　*

The sexual totem is also involved in the ceremonies of tribal initiation to adulthood.

The immature (of both sexes) are allowed to handle the father's sex totem, which is ceremonially marked with an L-shaped red symbol at both ends for the occasion. No immature female, or even immature male, is allowed abroad unchaperoned unless the initiation rites are surmounted. The ceremony is unpleasant but not mysterious, its details being proudly recounted by all survivors to their peer-group.

Once the young male has passed the initiation ceremony, he immediately takes possession of the father's sexual totem for his own reproductive activities. This illustration of the *Oedipus Complex* is striking. It should be noted that in the young suburbanite, both male and female, the sexual cycle is not restricted to week-ends but continues uninterruptedly.

The male begins his courtship activity by displaying his father's sexual totem (from which the red symbols are now removed) in every street of the village, to induce arousal in any female who happens to be about. Within a few days he will find a mate, particularly if the sexual totem is a large one.

Copulation takes place at night, in open country, generally under hedges, inside the father's sex totem. This is a widespread practice of which the significance still baffles psychologists.

By the process of completely *natural selection*, the new generation would choose their permanent mates from within the village, and from within the Young Conservatives. But like restless youth everywhere, most of our young now seek these partners far and wide. This is beneficial to our tribe's genetic health.

The suburbanite's genes resemble those of the fruit-fly *Drosophilia*, closely studied because of its quick breeding. Both suburbanite and fruit-fly can inherit abnormal genes, producing structural changes which accord them less success in stimulating females to mate. These are, in the fruit-fly (Aubrey Manning, loc. cit.),

(1) bar
(2) white
(3) forked and hairy
(4) vestigial and dumpy
(5) yellow and black.

In the suburbanite, (1) gives a propensity for drinking with the boys, (2) sedentary habits, (3) and (4) are self-obvious, and (5) is never seen.

Even the worse afflicted suburban young seem to find partners, and rarely suffer genetic death. Thus the equilibrium of our population is maintained. Marriages within the village are celebrated only in summer, amid enormous pomp and much feasting and drinking, and with all in tribal costume (*Moss Bros Effect*).

It is an interesting paradox that over the past two years the clan totem has tended to become larger, but the sexual totem much smaller.

*   *   *

A *taboo* (or *tabu*) is a tribal prohibition on certain objects, persons and activities — or even on reference to them in speech.

In suburbia we never mention, except with harmless humour, what we all know to be the driving force of our existence, which may be very beautiful, which may bring transcendent embellishment to our lives, yet may lead easily into the most sordid degeneration. Money.

No member of the tribe must know how much of it another member has got. Guesses are made, often shrewd, but accuracy is evasive through the pains and ingenuity of the tribesmen in concealing the truth. Generally, they make a pretence display which exaggerates their money, sometimes grossly so. The appurtenances of the abode are always priced to exclude the 20% cash-and-carry discount from the cut-price stores in Catford. Fine Fare is passed as Fortnums, Hepworths as Harrods.

All this is well understood by the tribeswomen, who appear at the abodes every week with small circular tins, supplicating alms. These are given with hearty generosity, but the sums of money accepted with touching gratitude by these poor women need never be substantial. If a man is importuned for a loan of any consequence, perhaps by another tribesman, or more likely by a male relative, he will assume a grievous demeanour and declare the amount temporarily beyond his resources. He may even, if tightly cornered, be obliged to tell the financial truth.

A *fetish* is some inanimate object believed (originally by the West African natives) to be imbued with magical powers. It may be for protection, or a source of dread.

Some suburbanites may be observed wearing a small copper amulet at the wrist. This is a fetish against disease, like the gallows' chips to ward off ague described by Sir Thomas Browne (1605–1682) in his *Pseudodoxia Epidemica (Vulgar Errors)* of 1646. It is curious that the talisman is never displayed by members of a lower social class. This may be from its cost, but more likely a sharpened cynicism.

The suburbanite is the only specimen extant who spends money on health. It is to be bought from numerous *Health Shops*, where it is dispensed as ill-favoured gruels solemnly consumed by the whole family at the morning feed. The only effect is increased   tivity of the bowels, which many suburban folk accept as synonymous with good health.

It is doubtful if the suburban people have real faith in these nostrums, because they turn to the medicine man in haste – even panic – if their health is genuinely disturbed, or they suspect it to be. If the medicine man fails to discover disease with his ju-ju, they never return contentedly to their folk-remedies. They demand to be taken into the presence of the Health God himself, *Bu-Pa*.

Bu-Pa is an interesting fetish. He is regarded

with ambivalence. His functions are protective, but obeisance to him is feared. All suburbanites make considerable sacrifices to *Bu-Pa*, and will defend him readily against attack. *Bu-Pa* may be another version of *Cerberus*, the monstrous dog in Greek mythology guarding the entrance to Hades. If regular sacrifices are not made to *Bu-Pa*, he lets the person through to a painful world known as *The Enachus*.

Fetishes against fire, robbery, flood, earthquake, rioting, nuclear radiation, even death itself, are conveniently combined in a yearly offering (which may be substantial) to the twin Junoesque goddesses, *Pearl* and *Pru*.

6 Suburban Culture

The suburban female has two hobbies, gynaecology and culture.

In suburbia, as Margaret Mead (b 1901) found in Samoa, 'Unlike her husband and brothers a woman spends most of her time within the narrower circle of her household and her relationship group.' She eases this confinement by attending to the *cultural current* which flows through the abode, about which the male exhibits as little concern or knowledge as about the mechanics of cooking his supper.

The cultural current circulates from the front door to the loft, like the centrally heated air. It may be as expensive to maintain. Its most substantial flotsam and jetsam are furnishings. Despite her fondness for pretence activity, the suburban female is commendably honest with herself. She admits that she possesses no taste. She must therefore go out and buy some, as she would buy garlic salt or tarragon vinegar.

Unfortunately, taste is costly and does not keep. The female may have originally furnished the abode from some reliable, traditional furniture company or massive store. She then enjoyed the misplaced confidence that the three-piece suite in cut moquette, the strongly patterned carpet, the walnut veneer bureau and stained oak refectory table with matching sideboard, the draped kidney dressing-table and candlewick bedcover, even the white furry nylon-topped stools, enjoyed the domestic durability of Stonehenge.

But fashion changes, infuriatingly and inexplicably (*Habitat's Law*). She had to fill the place with Finnish pine tables, Brazilian leather chairs, rush carpets from Tunisia, self-assembly Adam style Canadian pine mantels, Swedish glasswear, Danish cutlery and Hong Kong bamboo bottle-openers. She bought a Moroccan floormat as a bed-cover, but her husband rudely put it on the dog's basket.

The cultural current wafts the original furnishings up to the loft. When the loft becomes as crammed with serviceable household objects as a Pharoah's tomb, a shipment is made to Oxfam. Voyagers to this impoverished, sweltering and unhealthy country have noticed its wattle huts to be fitted comfortably with the products of The Times Furnishing Company.

This sample of taste, purchased so extravagantly, unhappily keeps no better than the first. The female is obliged to re-equip the abode with D-end pedestal dining-table and set of six tapestry-seated dining chairs including two carvers, Tudor telephone seat with guilloche motifs and Jacobean drinks cabinet, wing armchairs and genuine leather button-back chesterfield. These are conveniently produced in efficient factories, and may be inspected by the warehouseful.

The pendulum of history has swung with a speed that would have knocked Hepplewhite and Chippendale senseless. The painfully underprivileged, eternally perspiring and chronically sickly inhabitants of distant Oxfam have recently been baffled to unload cargoes of Italian Magestretti chairs, French non-stick omelette pans, Swiss fondu sets, English coachlamps, waxed-wood, ironware and cheap tin trays.

The female may be tempted to mount the pinnacle of taste by installing a sauna. But there are few of these to be found in BR1 2AX. They are difficult to insert between the back downstairs loo and the tumbler dryer, they put a terrible strain on the hot water bill and the prospect of all the neighbours in the nude is daunting.

The *bathroom*, which may or may not have a *sep*. *W C*, is a singularly anomalous place in the abode. It is the site of the family's most intimate activities, yet it must be freely open on Sunday mornings as part of the display activity. Failure to offer this unstinted hospitality may incite hostile tribal suspicion, like the holding of 'high tea'.

This paradox – a secret apartment periodically thrown open to the public – demands a high standard of sanitation. But the admirable ingenuity of the suburban female uses this forced exposure as a means of expressing the family's sophistication. This may otherwise be indicated by stuffed olives for Sunday drinks instead of cheese and onion flavour Golden Wonder crisps, duvets, indirect lighting, *Cosmopolitan* and a push-button telephone.

An electric toothbrush is a sure sign of worldliness. So is a bijou electric razor for the wife's superfluous. Carpeting is essential, right to the pedestal, thus creating a *luxury bath*. Some chronic crisis in the British paper industry has broken the heart of many a suburban female, by impairing the supply of matching loo paper.

The acme of suburban sophistication is possessing a bidet. The presence of this sanitary appliance is always discussed intently by visitors among themselves, and so is its function. I advise any couple moving into the suburbs, anxious for enduring and ungrudging social acclamation, that it can be achieved only be a *bidet fixe*.

In the sep. W C, air-wick is permissible, and devices which colour the water like squirts from a squid are passable. But not porcelain plaques with jokes, or *Here's The Wee Room* amid forget-me-nots on the door. Musical toilet-rolls are out, and musical seats definitely so.

Art in the abode wears better than the soft furnishings. Its changes are slow, if cruel. Paintings by the great, good St Peter Scott (b 1909), the St Francis of Assisi of the suburbs, have been swept away in the cultural current, displaced by Tretchikoff's *The Chinese Girl*. Those everlastingly ravenous natives in damp Oxfam now stare salivatingly at the plump fowls hanging thickly round their mud-caked walls. Some of this poultry was once depicted airborne in pottery on suburban walls, but they have long since flown off. A more testing cultural problem is offered by white ducks embossed on bright blue wallpaper, which is too expensive to remove. The shame can be hidden only by some large and awkward piece of furniture.

Art alone induces the male to venture his toe into the cultural current. The coloured print by Sir Russell Flint (1880–1969) is kept in the hall only through his encouragement. He says he knows it's art, because of all the tits. The male's cultural authority exists only in the garden, where the problems are pleasantly simple. In BR1 2AX, the gnome is extinct.

*　　　*　　　*

The female enjoys little time for active culture, after her devotional duties at the tribal totem and her domestic ones in the abode. Though *servants* have not been entirely eradicated from suburbia, particularly in the older houses.

Our maid of all work is not a servant, but attends us on a professional level, like the medicine man. We employ a jobbing gardener. Dear old Harold! A suburban man born and bred, ruddy-faced, portly, unshaven, home-made dog-end eternally drooping from his lower lip, the backbone of our nation.

We treat Harold like one of the family. When he arrives at the abode in the morning, he knows that he can go straight to the kitchen without the formality of invitation, to drink his coffee peacefully at the formica-topped table while munching his way through a packet of Viennas and reading our *Daily Express*. Then it's outside and down to work –

trimming the edges of the rose beds with the long-handled shears, watering the petunias, cutting a bunch of sweet-peas. He knocks off, for us to provide him with a midday repast and a couple of cans of Long Life, and we enjoy such mutual confidence that he can complain frankly about the choice or quality of the food should he feel like it.

Harold has a refreshing, earthy bluntness about him. He has no servile inhibitions about telling me, after I have performed some task in the garden during his absence, that I suppose I know I have 'done it all wrong'. Nor in refuting any contradiction to his views on the ways of plants and vegetables. At four o'clock, after his tea and a slice of Birdseye frozen cream sponge, he bids his gruff farewell and plods his weary way to the bus stop.

If Harold fills his pockets with small household items like matches, soap, toilet rolls or squeezees of Fairy Liquid – well, agricultural labourers were traditionally indulged to carry off a few of the Squire's apples and cherries. Harold insists on being paid in cash. He has a native craftiness under that simple exterior, and considerable distrust of the Inland Revenue.

I often reflect that if grander employers enjoyed the same relationship with their workforce as exists between Harold and myself, then the spiky problems of labour relations in this country would be solved. (A commercial friend in the City says that they do, and that's the trouble.)

We do not see much these days of young Arthur, Harold's son. Arthur is a cheerful young scamp, at present undergoing a training course at Borstal, after a bit of bad luck being caught one night poaching round the back of Woolworth's.

*   *   *

There is always *music* in the suburban home.

If the tribal totem is unwell, during the middle of the afternoon the female may deliberately tune the transistor to Radio Three. She may encounter with delighted recognition some piece of classical music written for one of the miracle plays which fill the T P Interval. But she finds that it does tend to go on rather. She is less concerned with her own musical education than that of her young. The musical talent of the suburban young must be brought as determinedly and honestly into the open as any of their secret bad habits. She therefore engineers the male into the purchase of a piano.

But the natives of suburbia have none of the natural rhythm enjoyed by those of West Africa, nor have their children the widespread aptitude for music noticed in those of the Polynesians by Captain Cook (1728–1779). Parents rapidly come to admit that their offspring are not budding Previns. A piano being an object far too valuable and bulky for dispatch to Oxfam – where it would usefully cheer Saturday night sing-songs round someone's discarded barbecue – it remains in the lounge unopened and untouched, silently expressing to visitors the glorious music of Beethoven, Mozart, Wagner and others which the family could, if they cared, extract from it.

Later, the children achieve unstinted musical

expression with the guitar, which requires no tuition nor ability for its performance, as may be heard in city streets and subways any day.

*   *   *

The literature of suburbia merits a monograph on its own.

In the pursuit of culture, reading strikes the female as an inexpensive and worthy activity. There are always books in the abode. The male takes pride in his splendid set of Sir Winston Churchill's (1874–1965), all in mint condition. There is the *Guinness Book of Records*, and she has the lovely poems of Sir John Betjeman (b 1906) and Mary Wilson (b 1916). BR1 2AX is not encyclopaedia-prospector's country.

But the world of literature is to the female as remote, mysterious, threatening – even frightening – as a thundercloud to a small child. She has no idea what she should be reading. Or more importantly, what she should be seen to be reading. Books are not discussed at Sunday drinks, and during coffee mornings only as merchandise. The suburbanites are practical beings, their days a complicated and wearisome struggle, their exhausted evenings passed in the recuperative lassitude of totemism. Books do not intrude into their lives more often, or more desiredly, than the attacks of influenza which occasion their reacquaintance.

The female finds guidance on a reading-list far more elusive than the guidance on sex which proliferates on all the bookstalls. Images occasionally

70

appear on the totem to educate the worshippers in a literary line. But they talk about persons she has never heard of, in a language imperfectly comprehensible. She turns hopefully to the more expensive Sunday papers, the presence of which on the doormat is itself a symbol of refined appreciation of all the better things in life.

The Sunday paper contains a catalogue of books which have been overbought by the booksellers and they wish to get rid of, known as 'The Bestseller List'. The female seeks wider information from the erudite reviewers occupying the rest of the page, but on reaching the conclusion that each is addressing only the others, she withdraws her eyes shyly, as though stumbling upon some private correspondence.

Neither are the advertisements edging the page much help in her selection. All the books recommend themselves with quotations of equally enthusiastic, unoriginal and similar praise. The female sighs despairingly, and turns to the more cheerful colour supplement. *There* she knows she will be more at home, amid the Sheraton-styled mahogany-veneered double-doored tribal totems, the wondrously swift and glittering sex totems, the distant lands of stintless sunshine, relaxation, excitement and brightly coloured seafood, the refrigerators that look like bank-vaults, and the drinks which conjure up parties of bewitchingly subdued vivacity and seductiveness.

Another advertisement suddenly holds her attention. It fills a whole page, in delightful colour. It is for books. Beautiful books, bound in real leather, or something quite closely resembling it, by those great

English authors like Dickens, Lamb, Shakespeare or Chaucer who are out of copyright, with real silk bookmark. She feels instantly and comfortably at home with this literary pronouncement. She sees that books are really pieces of furniture, like the reproduction Welsh glazed dresser with leaded windows and flute hand-carving on the opposite page.

The female cuts out the coupon with her matt-finished Finnish steel kitchen scissors. She turns the page to find yet another offer of books in this pressingly literate magazine. It appears that some cultured, erudite and kindly persons, gathering somewhere in north London, provide exactly the service required by unlettered, ill-educated, bemused suburban females like herself.

These littérateurs offer to choose a book for her reading once a month, like benign schoolteachers. They will go further. They will send her a book every month for an indefinite period, perhaps many years. They will also let her have, absolutely free of charge with her first volume, a small bust of Goethe in brown plastic. She notices that all the books will be restricted to the history, romance and practical application of sanitation – the scheme is entitled 'The Brain-Drain Book Club' – but feels that some of the volumes will doubtless prove of the highest interest.

Discovering that the enrolment cost is modest, the female cuts out this coupon as well. She anyway always cuts out coupons for everything, from life insurance and matching toilet cover with pedestal surround to careers in the Royal Navy and computer dating. She makes a nest of these in a small drawer of her rosewood-veneered bureau, from which they never emerge. This is another displacement activity, irrelevant behaviour in times of stress. It is perhaps related to the display of nesting material in the elaborate mating ritual of the female great-crested grebe (*Podiceps cristatus*), as described in 1914 by Sir Julian Huxley (1887–1975).

Some time during her life, the female will brave herself to venture into that temple of learning, a bookshop. She makes her way timidly past the magazines, paperclips, ballpoints, dinky toys, torch batteries, plastic bags, briefcases, foil freezer trays, records, paper napkins and sticks of plastic cups which fill the nave. With deepening reverence she enters the chancel, lined with paperbacks. She bows over the diminutive altar, with its precious offering of hardbacks.

She becomes too frightened to speak. Her eye runs along the faces of the paperbacks, all so neat, so clean, so identical, like hens in a battery. She recognizes an author's name or two. But she does not dare draw upon the wealth of our intellectual novelists, nor hear the momentous message of exiled Russians, though she thinks she ought to. She turns with relief to one of the novels written by the beautiful daughters of peers, which strike her as reliably genteel. Her hand is already outstretched, when she hears another purchaser of a paperback delivering a loud and condescending critique of the author to the bemused sixteen-year-old girl assistant – intellectual superiority is never acquired more cheaply than in

73

buying a book – and flees in panic from the temple, aghast at her own temerity.

The suburban male expresses robustly the discovery of the publisher Sir Stanley Unwin (1884–1968) – 'The average Englishman's idea that a book is a thing one begs, borrows, sometimes steals, but never buys except under compulsion.' The male sees starkly the ludicrousness of paying the same for one new novel as for two bottles of cut-price Scotch from St Augustine Barnett. He occasionally picks up at the station an enormous, sexy American paperback which has been read by everyone in the world, which the female takes when discarded and reads in bed, and greatly enjoys, to her credit.

7 Struggle for Existence

I have adopted the title of the third chapter in the work of Charles Darwin (1809–1882) *On the Origin of Species*.

The existence of the suburbanite is in jeopardy. Within a few years the species may become totally extinct, trampled to death by the Four Horsemen of the suburban Apocalypse, *Redundancy*, *Inflation*, *Taxation* and *Rateable Values*.

But life in the suburbs has always been hard. This is through the standard of living being dictated not by the male's economic circumstances, but by the standard of living of the others in the tribe (*Jones' Law*). As no one can know any male's exact economic resources, and by convention he is obliged to exaggerate them, existence in the suburbs can grow most complicated and testing. The accountancy problems alone are formidable.

But suburban man's anxieties are not simply financial. He worries about his health and takes up golf, then he worries about his game. He worries about everything in the abode, from the necessity of insulating the loft to that of taking the Dyno-Rod to the drains. He worries constantly about Rentokil. The words 'dry rot' occupy the same position in the suburbanite as Calais in Mary Tudor (1516–1558).

77

He worries about his children's passing their O-levels, and whether they might have a comprehensive education. He worries equally whether they will turn into hippies, or whether they will end with the same intolerably dreary commuting existence as himself. He worries whether his wife is having it off with the neighbours, and why he isn't having it off himself with the neighbours' wives (*Commandment Syndrome*). No wonder that every evening he offers grateful thanks to St Augustine Barnett.

The female has her own anxieties. She is tormented about slimming, like a devout but ravenous Mohammedan at midday in Ramadan. She worries about the concubines provided by the male's firm at his office. She worries that she will ever collect enough Green Shield stamps for the double caravan. She worries about using food beyond the shelf-life date. She worries that she is a suburban vegetable, like the marrows which flourish on the compost.

Instead of turning for solace to St Augustine Barnett, her reaction to these overwhelming fears is a wild urge to fly away. This is *escape behaviour*, induced by mounting anxiety, which may be observed particularly clearly in the differing postures of the agitated herring-gull (Manning, loc. cit.).

The female rarely does fly the abode, because this would be very inconvenient, involving writing directions for the milkman, getting another mother to pick up the children from school, leaving her suède-bound two-piece still at the cleaners, arranging baby-sitting, missing something on the tribal totem, etc.

Such intense psychological pressures naturally cause conflict in the abode. This occurs usually, though not exclusively, during the asexual phase, generally late at night or in early morning. It takes a ritual form, not unlike the mouth-fighting of the African cichlid fishes, who may end up by skinning each other.

The male invariably starts the conflict with a display of threatening behaviour. The female retaliates, making her own threat display. Physical contact is unusual, but there is a lot of noise. The conflict ends abruptly with the female's show of *appeasement activity*, taking a sitting posture with her legs extended and her hands covering her face, thus offering the aggressive male the most vulnerable parts of her body, like the female jackdaw baring the vital back of its neck to the male attacker's beak.

The male responds with his own appeasement display, placing his hands in his pockets, hunching his shoulders and scowling, the equivalent of the cock hiding away its provoking scarlet comb and wattles. The conflict is complicated by this male appeasement activity being so strongly desired by the female that she may deliberately have incited his aggression to that end. This is because the male appeasement may become elaborate, with flowers, gifts, ready permission to buy new clothes and visits to the theatre or restaurant. Without such appeasements by the male, some females eat away from the abode but once a year, at a firm function.

* * *

As with the mosquito-borne *plasmodium* parasite which causes malaria, the sexual phase of the suburbanite, too, can vary in length. At the winter solstice it is extended for several days. This is the time of the great workers' festival, similar to May Day.

The winter celebrations were originally confined to one day, but were extended by Sir John Lubbock (1834–1913) to two days in 1871. Over the past hundred years, the carnival has spread from the Thursday before to the Tuesday afterwards. In 1974, it was officially extended from the Thursday before until the morning of January 2, because the entire country becomes intoxicated on the night of December 31.

There are signs that, faced with the daunting prospect of work after so long a merrymaking, the entire country will become intoxicated again on the night of January 1, thus forcing the Government's hand and having the saturnalia prolonged to January 3, and then steadily onwards through the calendar until it joins up with the ten-day Fiesta at Easter, with nothing to stop it reaching the Summer Bank Holiday, mopping up Spring Bank Holiday on its way. There are many who believe this to be a painless way of solving the country's present economic and social problems.

The Workers' Winter Festival is celebrated in a subdued manner in suburbia. Male and female remain inside the abode, which is traditionally garnished in durable plastic. They spend most of the time piously worshipping the tribal totem and offering thanks to St Augustine Barnett.

In the summer months, the sexual phase of the suburbanite can last for weeks on end. The biological pressure grows so intense upon male and female cooped together in the abode, that only migration forestalls exhaustion.

Suburban migration is exactly the same as that of the birds, triggered by an instinctive desire for a higher temperature. To achieve this, a suburban family-group will thoughtlessly expose themselves to the gravest hazards of injury, infection, impure water and entirely unsuitable food. Yet many survive, and are to be seen in dense flocks, covering distant shores so thickly that the earth itself becomes invisible – a magnificent sight, compared by travellers to the massive penguin rookeries of Antarctica.

This irresistible urge towards bright sunlight is particularly marked in the British, because of the dank, misty and generally overcast native climate, and was responsible for the voyages of Drake, Raleigh, Cook and others, and the foundation of the British Empire (1757–1945).

*   *   *

And so we say goodbye to beautiful BR1 2AX.

I reach the end of my suburban safari in the reasonable hope that the species will survive, pruning its roses and planting its daffs, putting out its animals in the mornings and securing its abodes at night, existing unobtrusively in the sound of others' lawn mowers, the sight of others' airing smalls and the smell of others' compost. With only subdued and the politest comment, we watch each other arrive, breed, age and finally get taken away by Francis Chapell & Sons. We have learnt the art of living in gregarious isolation.

We shall survive because we go back to Chaucer (1340?–1400), who mentions the suburbs in his Prologue to the Yeoman's Tale, extremely rudely. We shall survive because we have in our veins the infinite ingenuity of Mr Pooter. We shall survive because the suburbs are extraordinarily pleasant places in which to live.

8 Elegy

ELEGY IN A SUBURBAN CHURCHYARD
Lines found scribbled on a torn bag of
National Growmore in a local potting shed.

The news at ten to six is on the box
The businessmen wind slowly from their trains,
The doors are opened promptly at 'The Fox',
I contemplate suburbia's sad remains.

A vulgar queue awaits a tardy bus
For transport to the pleasures of the night,
For bingo, films — beneath the likes of us
Who stay at home and stylishly get tight.

Suburbanites are comfortably superior
To dimmer aspirations of the masses,
Who holiday down-market in Iberia
Yet cannot tell a *ouzo* from a *cassis*.

Underneath this turf all men are equal.
The broker croaked, his clerk respectf'ly died.
Heritage of Earth is to the meek — well,
They still don't chat, forever side by side.

The lawyer predeceases his dear love
Full forty years before her ticker faltered.
'Reunited!' cries the stone set here above.
'My God,' he says, 'but darling, how you've
    altered.'

Some local Harold Wilson here may lie
Who for his country's governance never did,
Some toothless Heath, some Robin Day awry,
Some Twiggy unexploited 'neath her lid.

Virginia or Christine never seeded
Await eternal service 'neath this lawn,
Some Soper, some Muggeridge unheeded,
Some blushless Whitehouse, Longford lost to
    porn.

For them no more the heating's welcome fug
Or busy housewife's cherished evening *plat*,
No kids to spill their Scrabble on the rug,
Their coronaries quite put paid to that.

Our population's growing decimated,
I patronize the funerals — that I owe.
Some are planted, most just get cremated,
With a booze-up after on their patio.

Gravestones glimmer in the Council lighting,
No satin curtains draw to hide the night.
In drugless sleep they're for once delighting,
And every single one of them is white.

No melancholy vacuum e'er replaces
These stout suburban spirits quietly sped.
In BR1 2AX and suchlike places
It's all so dull we might right now be dead.

Bibliography

Bailey, C (1975), *Famous London Graves.*

Browne, Sir T (1646), *Pseudodoxia Epidemica.*

Chaucer, G (c 1385), *Canterbury Tales, Prologue to the Yeoman's Tale.*

Cook, J (1773), *An Account of a Voyage Round the World.*

Darwin, C (1859), *On the Origin of Species.*

Dickens, C J H (1837), *Pickwick Papers,* (1838), *Oliver Twist.*

Frazer, Sir J (1887), *Totemism.*

Freud, S (1913–14), *Totem and Taboo.*

Gauguin, P and Morice, C (1901), *Noa Noa.*

Gorer, G (1935), *Africa Dances.*

Huxley, Sir J (1914), *Proc. zool. Soc. Lond.,* 2, 491.

Manning, A (1972), *An Introduction to Animal Behaviour* (2nd ed.).

Maugham, W S (1938), *The Summing Up.*

Mead, M (1928), *Coming of Age in Samoa.*

Thomas, C G A (1973), *Medical Microbiology.* (3rd ed.).

Unwin, Sir S (1926), *The Truth About Publishing.*

White, G (1789), *The Natural History of Selborne.*